Symbols of Our Co...

I Sing the "Star-Spangled Banner"

Devon McKinney

illustrated by
Aurora Aguilera

PowerKiDS press

New York

Published in 2017 by The Rosen Publishing Group, Inc.
29 East 21st Street, New York, NY 10010

Copyright © 2017 by The Rosen Publishing Group, Inc.

All rights reserved. No part of this book may be reproduced in any form without permission in writing from the publisher, except by a reviewer.

First Edition

Managing Editor: Nathalie Beullens-Maoui
Editor: Caitie McAneney
Book Design: Michael Flynn
Illustrator: Aurora Aguilera

Library of Congress Cataloging-in-Publication Data

Names: McKinney, Devon, author.
Title: I sing the star-spangled banner / Devon McKinney.
Description: New York : PowerKids Press, 2017. | Series: Symbols of our
 country | Includes index.
Identifiers: LCCN 2016027415| ISBN 9781499427295 (pbk. book) | ISBN
 9781508153078 (6 pack) | ISBN 9781499427301 (library bound book)
Subjects: LCSH: Star-spangled banner (Song)–Juvenile literature. | National
 songs–United States–History and criticism–Juvenile literature. |
 Flags–United States–History–19th century–Juvenile literature.
Classification: LCC ML3561.S8 M4 2017 | DDC 782.42/15990973–dc23
LC record available at https://lccn.loc.gov/2016027415

Manufactured in the United States of America

CPSIA Compliance Information: Batch #BW17PK: For Further Information contact Rosen Publishing, New York, New York at 1-800-237-9932

Contents

Music Class	4
A Song from a Long Time Ago	14
We Sing with Pride	20
Words to Know	24
Index	24

I love music class. Today we're going to learn "The Star-Spangled Banner."

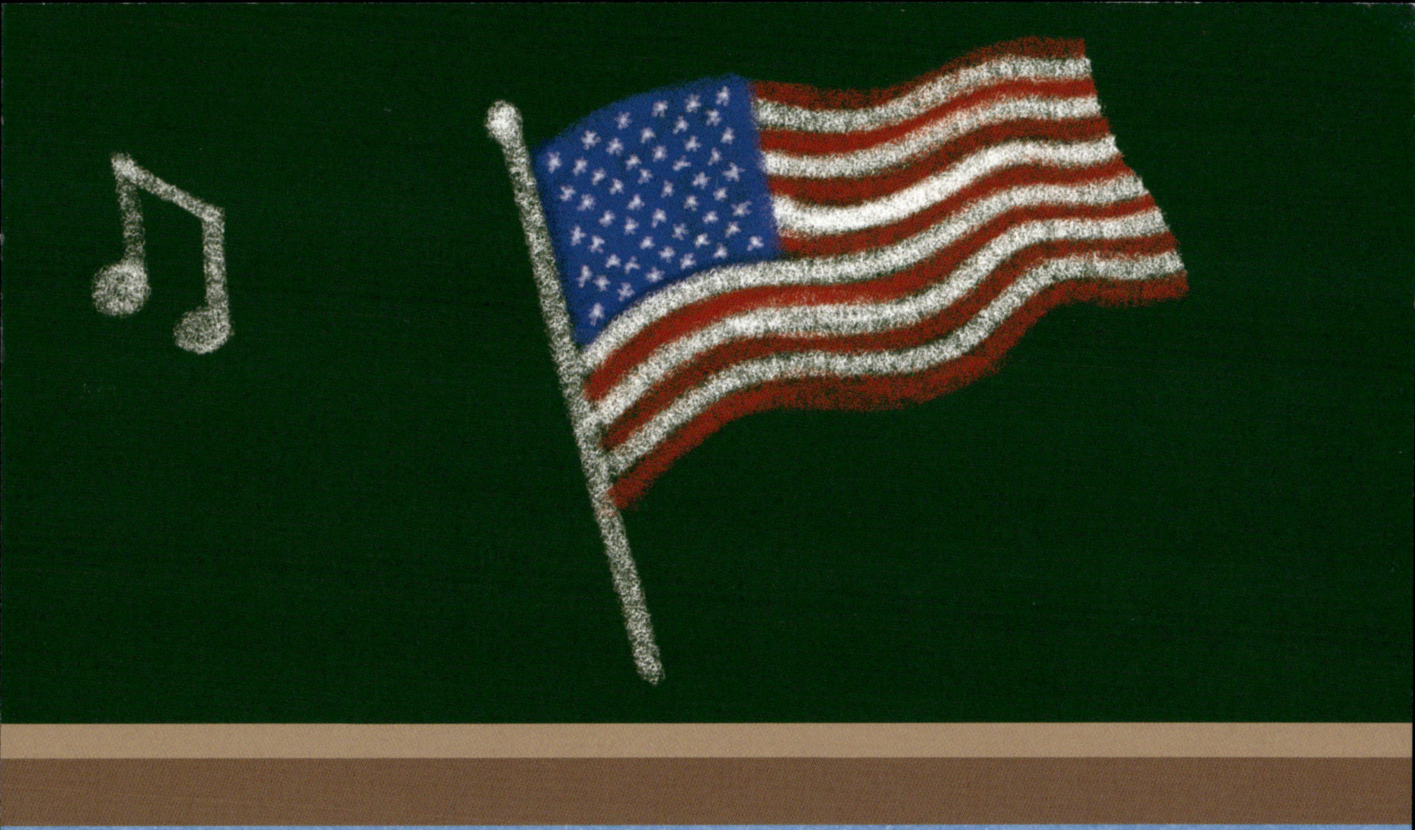

My teacher says this song is special.
It's our national anthem!

An anthem is the song of a nation. People sing it at important events.

I've heard this song before. People sing it before baseball games!

"Star-Spangled Banner"
is another name for the
American flag.

My teacher says the song was written a long time ago.

The poet was trapped on a boat during a battle. He watched for many hours.

Then, the poet saw an American flag flying above a fort. That meant the Americans won!

"The Star-Spangled Banner" tells the story of that great fight. We sing it proudly!

I loved singing our national anthem.

I can't wait to teach it to my friends!

Words to Know

American flag

boat

fort

Index

B
baseball, 10
battle, 17

N
national anthem, 7, 22

P
poet, 15, 17, 19

Made in United States
Orlando, FL
13 January 2022

About the Author

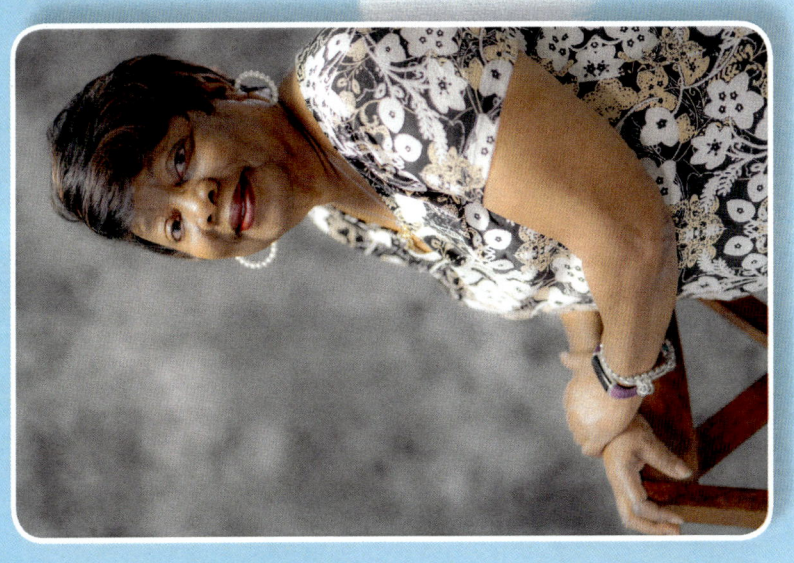

Geraldine McCall was born and raised in Pompano Beach, Florida, and now lives in Fort Lauderdale, Florida. She retired in 2005 from the Florida Department of Transportation after 32 years of service. She loves traveling, working at her church, and helping with Church Women United of Florida. She also enjoys gardening and gathering with friends and family.

Geraldine is the author of five other books which can be found at www.geraldinermccall.com

Diddy-Bite-You slept in Paula-Jean's room.

Mom leaned down to pick-up the toy, and Diddy-Bite-You licked her face and wagged his tail.
And that night when they went to bed ...

Diddy-Bite-You enjoyed the walk. Entering the den back home, he saw Mom and rushed to her, rubbing his body against her legs.

"You are still in need of a stern talk," Mom said.

"Momma, he is showing you that he is sorry. He is apologizing," Paula-Jean explained.

Mom looked at Diddy to see him standing on his hind legs turning in circles. Dropping to his feet, he ran to his toy box, picked up a toy and then ran back to Mom, placing the toy at her feet.

29

As they walked, Paula said to Deborah, "I didn't know that taking care of an animal would be so hard. Diddy keeps getting into trouble."
"He *is* only a puppy," Deborah replied.

He raised his large head and looked at Mom.
"Don't look at me with a sad face," Mom said. "It is outside for you tonight. You will be tied to the lemon tree."
Diddy-Bite-You continued to moan and began crawling towards Mom. Thinking quickly, Paula-Jean decided that mom needed time to cool down.
"Momma, please don't make him sleep outside," Paula-Jean begged. Without waiting for an answer, she said, "Come on, Diddy. I'm taking you for a walk to Deborah's house."

27

Entering the house, Paula-Jean dashed to the kitchen. On the countertop she saw the chewed remains of the steak.

Looking down she saw Diddy-Bite-You lying with his belly flat on the tile floor with his paws stretched past his large head. He began making whimpering sounds.

Shaking her finger, she said, "Diddy-Bite-You, you are a bad dog."

The next afternoon, Mom placed a steak on the kitchen counter to thaw. She then decided she needed a few items from the grocery store. Driving, Mom turned to Paula-Jean and said, "Oh my! I left the meat on the counter! What if Diddy-Bite-You sees it?" Paula-Jean said, "I don't think he will bother the meat Momma. You told him the kitchen was off limits." Mom answered, "If meat is left unguarded a dog will eat it." She immediately drove back home.

In the front yard, Diddy-Bite-You stood quietly, wagging his tail, while the girls dried him.

Diddy-Bite-You then ran toward the open front door but stopped in the middle of the living room. He shook water onto the coffee table, the sofa, and the lamp before running outside.

23

When it was time to leave the bathtub, Paula-Jean tugged on his leash to get him out of the water. He quickly jumped from the bathtub and shook water from his body. "No Diddy, don't shake inside, run outside! Deborah, will you open the front door for me?" Paula-Jean asked.

"Look!" Deborah exclaimed. "His tail is thumping from side-to-side." Diddy-Bite-You was patiently looking from Paula-Jean to Deborah while they soaped and scrubbed his fur. He quietly enjoyed his bath.

Deborah and Paula-Jean finally succeeded in getting him into the bathtub.
When they poured water over his fur, he sat with a thud.

He did not want to get into the bathtub and began to pull back. Putting a leash around his neck, Paula-Jean said. "I have to bathe you before Mom sees you." Diddy-Bite-You again tried to pull away.

Paula-Jean and Deborah did not wait. When Diddy-Bite-You saw them leaving, he quickly followed.

When they got to a large puddle of water, Diddy-Bite-You dropped to the ground and rolled around in it. His hairy coat was covered with mud.

"Diddy-Bite-You, get out of that water!" Paula-Jean scolded. But Diddy continued rolling back and forth. Shaking a finger at him, Paula-Jean said, "Come on! I must bathe you before Mom sees how dirty you are, and makes you sleep outside."

Diddy-Bite-You pranced as he followed them home.

"No!" Paula-Jean yelled. "Diddy-Bite-You, come back here!" The squirrel ran up the tree and Diddy-Bite-You stood on his hind legs, barking.

It began to rain as they walked. "Hurry," Deborah said. They started to run. Instead of following the girls, Diddy-Bite-You ran after a large tree squirrel that had an acorn in its mouth.

"Diddy-Bite-You, stop that!" Paula-Jean said as she and Deborah climbed from the tree. "I should have put his new leash on him. We are leaving."

Several peahens and peafowl were pecking the ground. Suddenly the peacock was between the peahens and Diddy-Bite-You. The peacock turned and ran towards the puppy!

The peacock was protecting the hens and fowl.

"Look!" Deborah shouted. "The peacock is protecting the hens and fowl!"

Diddy-Bite-You was running in circles, barking at a peacock. The peacock's under belly was an iridescent shade of blue. Its tail feathers were radiant. The colors were turquoise, blue, orange, and green. The feathers were spread wide and tall, and bounced gracefully as the peacock strutted between the pine trees.

Meanwhile, Diddy-Bite-You rummaged through the underbrush. In moments, the girls' attention was interrupted by barking.

"Why are you making so much noise?" Paula-Jean demanded.

Paula-Jean and Deborah loved climbing trees in the nearby wooded area. From the tallest pine tree, they often sat on a limb watching what was happening in the neighborhood. The neighborhood boys had a 'boys only' camp. Today the girls saw them playing a lively game of touch football. They also heard the yells and screams from where they were.

11

When Paula-Jean returned home from school, she could see Diddy-Bite-You in the window wagging his tail. At night she told him about her day as he lay on her bed before falling asleep.

Deborah lived two houses away from Paula-Jean and was her best friend.

The three became inseparable. Paula-Jean and Deborah taught Diddy-Bite-You how to fetch a ball, how to sit on command, and how to walk on his hind legs.

"Dad, can I take him to Deborah's house? I want her to see my new dog."

"Be careful walking him," he replied. "There is no leash law, but I intend to get one for him. Make sure he doesn't run into traffic."

Mom said, "Should he be kept outside or inside? I'm not sure about him sleeping inside."

"Momma, please! I want him to sleep in my room with me, please, please!" Paula-Jean whined.

"We will give it a try," Mom reluctantly agreed.

Her dad smiled. "What are you going to name him?"
"You named him! His name is Diddy-Bite-You."
"That is a question, not a name for a dog," her dad replied.
"He likes it. Look at his tail wag," Paula-Jean insisted.

Paula-Jean patted the dog on his head. He nipped her hand. "Oh my gosh, did he bite you?" dad asked. "I may have to take him back."
"No Dad, he didn't bite me." Paula-Jean hugged the puppy. "He kissed me!"

A large puppy bounded into the living room. He was a mixture of Airedale and German Shepherd. His semi-long hair was white, brown, and grey. His head, ears, and paws were larger than those of any other dog his age.

"A puppy!" Paula-Jean exclaimed.

"Well, you're seven and we think you are ready to take care of a dog," dad said.

Dedication

This book is dedicated to all children who love to read.

Text ©2021 by Geraldine McCall
Illustrations ©2021 by Melanie Mitchell

Photo of Geraldine McCall by Karen Roberts

Published by Miriam Laundry Publishing Company
miriamlaundry.com

All rights reserved. This book or any portion thereof may not be reproduced or used in any manner whatsoever without the express written permission from the author except for the use of brief quotations in a book review.

PB ISBN 978-1-990107-16-0
e-Book ISBN 978-1-990107-17-7

Printed in USA   FIRST EDITION

Paula-Jean and Diddy-Bite-You

Written by
Geraldine McCall

Illustrated by
Melanie Mitchell